BLIK BOOKS

FOR THE BETTER

Illustrated by Katerina Grik

Grief Relief no.2
Coloring Book

This book belongs to

_____

Date

_____

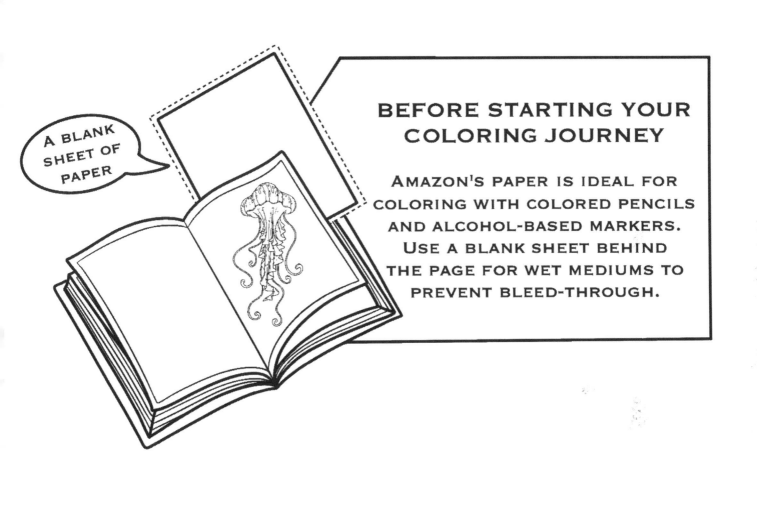

A BLANK SHEET OF PAPER

BEFORE STARTING YOUR COLORING JOURNEY

AMAZON'S PAPER IS IDEAL FOR COLORING WITH COLORED PENCILS AND ALCOHOL-BASED MARKERS. USE A BLANK SHEET BEHIND THE PAGE FOR WET MEDIUMS TO PREVENT BLEED-THROUGH.

A BLANK SHEET OF PAPER

BEFORE STARTING YOUR COLORING JOURNEY

AMAZON'S PAPER IS IDEAL FOR COLORING WITH COLORED PENCILS AND ALCOHOL-BASED MARKERS. USE A BLANK SHEET BEHIND THE PAGE FOR WET MEDIUMS TO PREVENT BLEED-THROUGH.

Color Testing Pages

Obsessed with the coloring pages in this book?

Thank you for your Amazon review and supporting Blik Books!

Enjoy *5 FREE* exclusive coloring pages as our token of appreciation!

Simply DM *@BLIKBOOKS* on Instagram and drop your email to

receive your complimentary PDF!

BLIK BOOKS

FOR THE BETTER

A Journey of Healing and Self-Discovery

In times of loss, we're flooded with various emotions, from sorrow to solitude. Yet, within the darkness, hope emerges. Throughout this journey, we learn that acknowledging our feelings, expressing ourselves creatively, and seeking support are vital for healing and growth. Come with us as we explore how embracing sadness and engaging in mindful activities such as coloring, writing, and self-reflection can transform our lives.

GRIEF IS A NATURAL RESPONSE TO LOSS: A journey we all must traverse at some point in our lives. It's a complex emotional state that can leave us feeling overwhelmed, lost, and utterly alone. However, amidst the darkness, there are rays of hope and avenues for healing waiting to be explored.

EMBRACING GRIEF AS A NATURAL RESPONSE: Contrary to societal norms, grief is not a sign of weakness but a testament to the depth of our love and connection. It's essential to embrace grief as an integral part of our healing journey rather than suppress it.

COLORING AS MEDITATION: Engaging in coloring activities can be a form of meditation that calms the mind and soothes the soul. As we immerse ourselves in the rhythm of coloring, our worries fade away, and we find solace in the present moment.

USING COLORS TO EXPRESS EMOTIONS: Choose colors that resonate with your emotions - dark shades for sorrow, bright hues for hope. Let your intuition guide you as you navigate the spectrum of your feelings. Look at art to get inspired.

WRITING AS A TOOL FOR PROCESSING: Writing about your feelings can help you process them better. Use the journal pages to express yourself freely, allowing your words to flow without judgment or inhibition.

ACCEPTANCE OF NOT BEING OKAY: It's okay not to be okay sometimes. Give yourself permission to feel whatever emotions arise without guilt or shame.

TAKING ONE DAY AT A TIME: Grief doesn't have an expiration date. Take each day as it comes, allowing yourself the space and time to heal at your own pace.

MINDFUL COLORING: Don't rush through the coloring pages. Take your time and let your emotions guide you as you explore the intricate patterns and designs.

MANDALAS FOR INNER PEACE: Coloring mandalas can bring about inner peace and balance in times of distress. The circular patterns symbolize unity and wholeness, reminding us of the interconnectedness of all things.

SCIENTIFIC VALIDATION: Studies have shown that coloring complex geometric patterns reduces anxiety levels, offering tangible evidence of the therapeutic benefits of this practice.

ALLOWING YOURSELF TO FEEL: The only way out is through. Allow yourself to feel every emotion fully before moving on to the next stage of grief. Avoidance only prolongs the healing process.

THERAPEUTIC WRITING: Write letters to your lost loved ones in the journal pages. It's a cathartic practice that allows you to express your thoughts and feelings in a safe and nurturing environment.

INDIVIDUAL PATHS TO HEALING: There's no right or wrong way to grieve. Each person's journey is unique, and it's essential to honor and respect your own process.

CREATING A SAFE SPACE: Surround yourself with comfort while coloring - light candles, play soothing music, and ensure you're in a cozy environment that fosters relaxation and introspection.

COLORING AS SELF-REFLECTION: Coloring is not just an activity; it's an opportunity for self-reflection and introspection. Pay attention to the thoughts and feelings that arise as you engage in this creative process.

EMBRACING IMPERFECTION: There are no mistakes in art. If you color outside the lines or choose unconventional colors, it's all part of expressing yourself authentically.

SEEKING SUPPORT: You don't have to face grief alone. Share your journey with trusted friends or family members who understand what you're going through. Their presence and support can provide immense comfort and solace.

COURAGE IN HEALING: Healing takes courage, but we all have the strength within us to embark on this journey of self-discovery and renewal. Trust in your resilience and inner power to guide you through the darkest of times.

PRESENT MOMENT AWARENESS: Coloring helps us focus on the present moment, alleviating feelings of anxiety or depression that may accompany grief. By grounding ourselves in the here and now, we find peace and clarity amidst the chaos.

"It's just a bad day, not a bad life." — Anonymous

"The emotion that can break your heart is sometimes the very one that heals it." – Nicholas Sparks

"Don't cry when the sun is gone because the tears won't let you see the stars." — Violeta Parra

"Hearts live by being wounded." — Oscar Wilde

"Our greatest glory is not in never falling, but in rising every time we fall." — Confucius

"Sadness gives depth. Happiness gives height.
Sadness gives roots.
Happiness gives branches." — Osho

"Turn your wounds into wisdom." — Oprah Winfrey

"You yourself, as much as anybody in the entire universe deserve your love and affection" — Buddha

"You may encounter many defeats, but you must not be defeated. In fact, it may be necessary to encounter the defeats, so you can know who you are, what you can rise from, how you can still come out of it."
— Maya Angelou

"Life isn't about waiting for the storm to pass...
It's about learning to dance in the rain"
— Vivian Greene

"There is no remedy for love but to love more."
— Henry David Thoreau

"It's amazing how someone can break your heart and you can still love them with all the little pieces."
— Ella Harper

"Every time your heart is broken, a doorway cracks open to a world full of new beginnings, new opportunities." — Patti Roberts

"When one door of happiness closes, another opens —
but often we look so long at the closed door that we do
not see the one which has been opened for us."
— Helen Keller

"The reality is you will grieve forever. You will not get over the loss of a loved one: you will learn to live with it. You will heal and you will rebuild yourself around the loss you have suffered. You will be whole again, but you will never be the same. Nor should you be the same, nor would you want to."

— Elisabeth Kübler-Ross

"You have to be unique, and different, and shine in your own way." – Lady Gaga

"To be creative means to be in love with life." — Osho

"The risk of love is loss, and the price of loss is grief. But the pain of grief Is only a shadow when compared with the pain of never risking love."
— Hilary Stanton Zunin

"Sometimes, only one person is missing, and the whole world seems depopulated."

— Alphonse de Lamartine

"Only people who are capable of loving strongly can also suffer great sorrow, but this same necessity of loving serves to counteract their grief and heals them." — Leo Tolstoy

"To weep is to make less the depth of grief."
— William Shakespeare

"No one ever told me that grief felt so like fear."

— C.S Lew

"Grief can be a burden, and an anchor. You get used to the weight, how it holds you in place." — Sarah Dessen

Remember: "You are braver than you believe, stronger than you seem, smarter than you think and loved more than you know" – A.A. Milne

"It's okay not to be okay all the time."

— Selena Gomez

"Healing takes courage, and we all have courage, even if we have to dig a little to find it." — Tori Amos

"Grief is like the ocean — it comes in waves, ebbing and flowing. Sometimes the water is calm, and sometimes it is overwhelming. All we can do is learn to swim." — Vicki Harrison

"The reality is that you will grieve forever. You will not get over the loss of a loved one — you will learn to live with it." — Elisabeth Kubler-Ross

"This too shall pass" — Persian Sufi Poets

"Grief never ends... But it changes. It's a passage, not a place to stay. Grief is not a sign of weakness, nor a lack of faith...

It is the price of love." — Unknown

"The pain passes,

but the beauty stays." — Pierre Auguste Renoir

"It's not what you look at that matters, it's what you see" – Henry David Thoreau

"The wound is the place where the Light enters you." – Rumi

"In the process of letting go you will lose many things from the past, but you will find yourself." — Deepak Chopra

SOME EXAMPLES WHAT TO WRITE ABOUT IN THESE JOURNALING PAGES:

REFLECT ON YOUR DAY: WHAT WERE THE HIGHLIGHTS? WHAT CHALLENGES DID YOU FACE? WRITE ABOUT A GOAL YOU'RE WORKING TOWARDS AND THE PROGRESS YOU'VE MADE. LIST THINGS YOU APPRECIATE ABOUT YOURSELF. DESCRIBE A PLACE THAT BRINGS YOU PEACE OR INSPIRES YOU. SHARE A RECENT ACCOMPLISHMENT AND HOW IT MADE YOU FEEL. REMEMBER, THERE'S NO RIGHT OR WRONG WAY TO JOURNAL. IT'S A PERSONAL PRACTICE AND SHOULD BE TAILORED TO SUIT YOUR NEEDS AND PREFERENCES.

ACCORDING TO PSYCHOLOGY TODAY, SHARING STORIES ABOUT YOUR LOST BELOVED ONE CAN HELP KEEP THEIR MEMORY ALIVE AND HELP WITH THE GRIEVING PROCESS. WHICH STORIES AND MEMORIES CAN YOU WRITE ABOUT?

REFLECT ON HOW COLORING A DESIGN IN THIS COLORING BOOK EACH DAY OR WEEK HAS INFLUENCED YOUR MOOD AND MINDSET. HOW DO YOU FEEL NOW COMPARED TO WHEN YOU STARTED THIS DAILY PRACTICE? WE HOPE YOU FEEL BETTER AND WISH YOU ALL THE BEST!

REFLECT ON A RECENT CHALLENGE OR DILEMMA YOU FACED. HOW MIGHT ADOPTING CLINICAL PSYCHOLOGIST JORDAN PETERSON'S APPROACH OF WRITING AS IF CONVERSING WITH SOMEONE ELSE ENHANCE YOUR ABILITY TO ORGANIZE YOUR THOUGHTS AND GAIN CLARITY ON THE SITUATION? EXPLORE THE BENEFITS OF THIS WRITING TECHNIQUE FOR PROBLEM-SOLVING AND SELF-REFLECTION. THEN TRY TO SHARE THESE WORDS WITH SOMEONE CLOSE TO YOU.

WRITE A LETTER TO YOUR FUTURE SELF. WHAT ADVICE WOULD YOU GIVE
YOURSELF? WHAT HOPES DO YOU HAVE FOR THIS PERSON?
WHAT ARE YOUR DREAMS, BIG AND SMALL?

SPEND SOME TIME REFLECTING ON ANY OBSTACLES NOW STANDING IN YOUR WAY. HOW MIGHT THEY BE OVERCOME?

JOT DOWN A FEW MEMORIES THAT COME TO MIND AND SHARE YOUR CURRENT
FEELINGS ABOUT THEM.

"HAPPINESS IS NOT SOMETHING READY MADE. IT COMES FROM YOUR OWN ACTIONS."
– DALAI LAMA XIV

REFLECT ON A TIME WHEN YOUR ACTIONS DIRECTLY CONTRIBUTED TO YOUR HAPPINESS. HOW DID YOUR CHOICES AND BEHAVIORS INFLUENCE YOUR EMOTIONAL WELL-BEING? SHARE AN EXPERIENCE WHERE YOU REALIZED THAT HAPPINESS IS A RESULT OF YOUR OWN ACTIONS, AS EXEMPLIFIED BY THIS QUOTE.

WRITE ABOUT WHAT STARTING A NEW LIFE MEANS TO YOU. WHAT WOULD IT LOOK LIKE?
WHAT STEPS COULD YOU TAKE TOWARDS IT?

"THE GREATEST GLORY IN LIVING LIES NOT IN NEVER FALLING, BUT IN RISING EVERY TIME WE FALL." - NELSON MANDELA.
HOW DOES NELSON MANDELA'S QUOTE RESONATE WITH YOUR OWN EXPERIENCES OF OVERCOMING ADVERSITY AND BOUNCING BACK FROM SETBACKS IN LIFE?

"THE BEST WAY OUT IS ALWAYS THROUGH."- ROBERT FROST.THIS QUOTE ENCOURAGES US TO FACE OUR PROBLEMS HEAD-ON RATHER THAN AVOIDING THEM.
REFLECT ON A TIME WHEN YOU CONFRONTED A CHALLENGE HEAD-ON INSTEAD OF AVOIDING IT. WHAT DID YOU LEARN FROM THIS EXPERIENCE, AND HOW DID IT SHAPE YOUR APPROACH TO OVERCOMING OBSTACLES IN THE FUTURE?"
TIP: WRITE ABOUT YOUR FEELINGS WITHOUT JUDGMENT OR ANALYSIS. THIS CAN HELP YOU PROCESS EMOTIONS AND REDUCE FEELINGS OF SADNESS.

SPEND SOME TIME MEDITATING THEN WRITE DOWN ANY INSIGHTS OR FEELINGS
THAT AROSE DURING YOUR PRACTICE.

PRACTICE GRATITUDE BY LISTING THREE THINGS YOU'RE THANKFUL FOR EACH MORNING IN
YOUR JOURNAL. THIS COULD ALREADY BE A DELIGHTFUL CUP OF COFFEE,
THE BEAUTIFUL SKY, YOUR HEALTH, WHATEVER.

"YOU DON'T HAVE TO SEE THE WHOLE STAIRCASE, JUST TAKE THE FIRST STEP."
– MARTIN LUTHER KING JR.,
ENCOURAGING US TO START ANEW WITHOUT HAVING ALL ANSWERS BEFOREHAND.

REFLECT ON A MOMENT WHEN YOU FELT TRULY ALIVE AND INSPIRED
- WHAT WERE YOU DOING? WHO WERE YOU WITH?

INCORPORATE MINDFULNESS EXERCISES INTO YOUR JOURNALING ROUTINE, SUCH AS DEEP BREATHING OR PROGRESSIVE MUSCLE RELAXATION. PROGRESSIVE MUSCLE RELAXATION (PMR) IS A RELAXATION METHOD WHERE YOU TENSE AND THEN RELAX DIFFERENT MUSCLE GROUPS TO REDUCE OVERALL TENSION AND PROMOTE RELAXATION.

"IN THE MIDST OF WINTER, I FOUND THERE WAS WITHIN ME AN INVINCIBLE SUMMER." - ALBERT CAMUS.
USE THIS QUOTE AS INSPIRATION WHEN WRITING ABOUT OVERCOMING SADNESS OR ADVERSITY.

WRITE A LETTER TO A LOVED ONE YOU'VE LOST, EXPRESSING EVERYTHING YOU WISH YOU COULD TELL THEM NOW. HOW DO YOU FEEL NOW?

HOW INCREDIBLE IS IT THAT JUST 45 MINUTES OF CREATIVE ACTIVITY CAN MAKE SUCH A SIGNIFICANT DIFFERENCE IN REDUCING STRESS LEVELS? IT'S EMPOWERING TO KNOW THAT REGARDLESS OF ARTISTIC BACKGROUND OR SKILL, ENGAGING IN CREATIVE PURSUITS CAN HAVE SUCH A PROFOUND IMPACT ON OUR WELL-BEING.

DEDICATE ONE PAGE OF YOUR JOURNAL FOR POSITIVE AFFIRMATIONS – STATEMENTS THAT ENCOURAGE POSITIVITY AND SELF-BELIEF. SOME EXAMPLES:

"I TRUST IN MY ABILITY TO OVERCOME CHALLENGES."

"I AM DESERVING OF HAPPINESS AND SUCCESS."

"I EMBRACE MY UNIQUENESS AND CELEBRATE MY INDIVIDUALITY."

"I AM SURROUNDED BY LOVE AND SUPPORT."

"I AM RESILIENT AND CAPABLE OF ADAPTING TO CHANGE."

"I AM GRATEFUL FOR THE OPPORTUNITIES LIFE PRESENTS TO ME."

"When one door of happiness closes, another opens — but often we look so long at the closed door that we do not see the one which has been opened for us."
— Helen Keller

Sources

Quotes

Here's the text formatted neatly for your book formatter:

- Quote: "What we once enjoyed and deeply loved we can never lose, for all that we love deeply becomes part of us."
  - Source: Keller, Helen. *We Bereaved*. 1929

- Quote: "In the process of letting go you will lose many things from the past, but you will find yourself."
  - Source: Chopra, Deepak. *The Book of Secrets: Unlocking the Hidden Dimensions of Your Life*. 2004.

- Quote: "Remember: You are braver than you believe, stronger than you seem, smarter than you think and loved more than you know."
  - Source: Milne, A.A. *Winnie-the-Pooh*.

- Quote: "The wound is the place where the Light enters you."
  - Source: Rumi, often attributed to various translations of his poetry.

- Quote: "It's not what you look at that matters, it's what you see."
  - Source: Thoreau, Henry David. *Journal*, 1851.

- Quote: "It's okay not to be okay all the time."
  - Source: Gomez, Selena. Public statements or interviews.

- Quote: "The pain passes, but the beauty stays."
  - Source: Renoir, Pierre Auguste. Commonly attributed to his views on art and suffering.

- Quote: "Grief never ends... But it changes. It's a passage, not a place to stay. Grief is not a sign of weakness, nor a lack of faith... It is the price of love."
  - Source: This quote is widely circulated without a definitive source.

- Quote: "This too shall pass."
  - Source: Attributed to Persian Sufi poets, a common phrase in Persian literature.

- Quote: "The reality is that you will grieve forever. You will not 'get over' the loss of a loved one - you will learn to live with it."
  - Source: Kübler-Ross, Elisabeth. *On Grief and Grieving*. 2005.

- Quote: "You have to be unique, and different, and shine in your own way."
  - Source: Gaga, Lady. Public statements or interviews.

- Quote: "Grief is like the ocean - it comes in waves, ebbing and flowing. Sometimes the water is calm, and sometimes it is overwhelming. All we can do is learn to swim."
  - Source: Harrison, Vicki. Often quoted in grief literature.

- Quote: "Healing takes courage, and we all have courage, even if we have to dig a little to find it."
  - Source: Amos, Tori. Public statements or interviews.

- Quote: "To be creative means to be in love with life."
  - Source: Osho. Various writings and lectures.

- Quote: "Grief can be a burden, and an anchor. You get used to the weight, how it holds you in place."
  - Source: Dessen, Sarah. *The Truth About Forever*. 2004.

- Quote: "No one ever told me that grief felt so like fear."
  - Source: Lewis, C.S. *A Grief Observed*. 1961.

- Quote: "To weep is to make less the depth of grief."
  - Source: Shakespeare, William. *King Henry VI*.

- Quote: "Only people who are capable of loving strongly can also suffer great sorrow, but this same necessity of loving serves to counteract their grief and heals them."
  - Source: Tolstoy, Leo. *War and Peace*. 1869.

- Quote: "Sometimes, only one person is missing, and the whole world seems depopulated."
  - Source: Lamartine, Alphonse de. *Méditations poétiques*. 1820.

- Quote: "The only way to deal with pain is to transform it into something that can nourish others."
  - Source: Weil, Simone. Various writings.

- Quote: "When one door of happiness closes, another opens - but often we look so long at the closed door that we do not see the one which has been opened for us."
  - Source: Keller, Helen. *We Bereaved*. 1929

- Quote: "Every time your heart is broken, a doorway cracks open to a world full of new beginnings, new opportunities."
  - Source: Roberts, Patti. *Paradox - The Angels Are Here*. 2010.

- Quote: "Sometimes good things fall apart so better things can fall together."
  - Source: Monroe, Marilyn. Commonly attributed to her statements.

- Quote: "It's amazing how someone can break your heart and you can still love them with all the little pieces."
  - Source: Harper, Ella. *Pieces of You*. 2013.

- Quote: "There is no remedy for love but to love more."
  - Source: Thoreau, Henry David. *Journal*, 1852.

- Quote: "Life isn't about waiting for the storm to pass… It's about learning to dance in the rain."
  - Source: Greene, Vivian. Various works.

- Quote: "You may encounter many defeats, but you must not be defeated. In fact, it may be necessary to encounter the defeats, so you can know who you are, what you can rise from, how you can still come out of it."
  - Source: Angelou, Maya. *Letter to My Daughter*. 2008.

- Quote: "You yourself, as much as anybody in the entire universe deserve your love and affection."
  - Source: Attributed to Buddha, various teachings.

- Quote: "Turn your wounds into wisdom."
  - Source: Winfrey, Oprah. Public statements or interviews.

- Quote: "Sadness gives depth. Happiness gives height. Sadness gives roots. Happiness gives branches."
  - Source: Osho. Various writings and lectures.

- Quote: "Our greatest glory is not in never falling, but in rising every time we fall."
  - Source: Attributed to Confucius, various teachings.

- Quote: "Hearts live by being wounded."
  - Source: Wilde, Oscar. *De Profundis*. 1905.

- Quote: "Don't cry when the sun is gone because the tears won't let you see the stars."
  - Source: Attributed to Violeta Parra, various works.

- Quote: "The emotion that can break your heart is sometimes the very one that heals it."
  - Source: Sparks, Nicholas. *At First Sight*. 2005.

Prompts Journaling Pages

Camus, Albert. *Return to Tipasa*. 1954.
King Jr., Martin Luther. *Stride Toward Freedom: The Montgomery Story*. 1958.
Frost, Robert. *A Servant to Servants*. 1914.
Mandela, Nelson. *Long Walk to Freedom*. 1994.
Dalai Lama XIV. *The Art of Happiness*. 1998.
Psychology Today. "Sharing Stories of Lost Loved Ones and Memory." Psychology Today, [Link to article].
Journal of Positive Psychology. "Effects of Creative Activities on Stress Reduction." [Link to article].
Clinical Psychology Review. "Progressive Muscle Relaxation Techniques and Benefits." [Link to article].
Peterson, Jordan B. *12 Rules for Life: An Antidote to Chaos*. 2018.